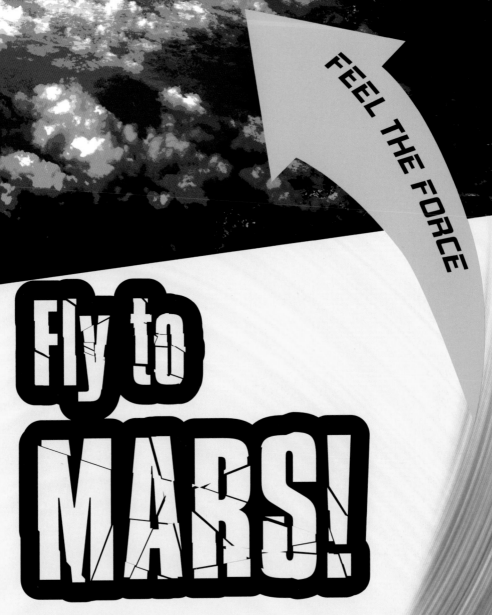

Fly to MARS!

Forces in Space

Richard and Louise Spilsbury

Heinemann raintree

Edited by Helen Cox Cannons and Holly Beaumont
Designed by Philippa Jenkins
Original illustrations © Capstone Global Library Ltd
Illustrated by HL Studios, Witney, Oxon, England
Picture research by Tracy Cummins
Production by Helen McCreath
Originated by Capstone Global Library Ltd
Printed and Bound in China by Leo Paper Group

19 18 17 16 15
10 9 8 7 6 5 4 3 2 1

Library of Congress Cataloging-in-Publication Data
Cataloging-in-publication data is available at the Library of Congress.
ISBN 978-1-4846-2600-9 (hardback)
ISBN 978-1-4846-2605-4 (paperback)
ISBN 978-1-4846-2615-3 (ebook PDF)

Acknowledgments
We would like to thank the following for permission to reproduce photographs: Capstone Press: 31, HL Studios, 9, 17, 29, 35, Karon Dubke, 10, 11, 24, 25, 36, 37; Corbis: REUTERS/Sergei Remezov, 13, Tsolo T. Tsolo/Science Faction, 14; Getty Images: The Asahi Shimbun, 15; NASA: Bill Ingalls, 4, 7, Front Cover, Johnson Space Center, 19, 20, 21, 23, 26, 27, 43 Bottom, JPL-Caltech, 33, 34, 38, Victor Zelentsov, 12; Science Source: Detlev van Ravenswaay, 41; Shutterstock: iurii, 43 Top, Jacek Chabraszewski, 42 Top, Keith Tarrier, 42 Bottom, musicman, 43 Top, solarseven, Design Element, Twin Design, 5, vnlit, 42 Middle; Thinkstock: 3DSculptor, 18.

We would like to thank Patrick O'Mahony for his invaluable help in the preparation of this book.

Every effort has been made to contact copyright holders of material reproduced in this book. Any omissions will be rectified in subsequent printings if notice is given to the publisher.

Contents

Some words are shown in bold, **like this**. You can find
out what they mean by looking in the glossary.

Why Do We Go into Space?

Human beings always want to know more. That's one reason people explore space: to know what is out there. As the world's population grows, space exploration might also help us. Explorers might find another planet that humans could live on or discover **resources** that could help us solve problems on Earth.

Space exploration

The first objects to travel to and explore space were **satellites**, in 1957. Since then, people have flown on spacecraft and even walked on the Moon. Today, there are even space stations where people can live and study space high above Earth. These missions into space are only possible because people have created machines that use incredible **forces** to carry spacecraft away from Earth.

Why Mars?

Small spacecraft have been flying near and visiting Mars for decades, but in the future, people hope to go there. Mars is the planet that most resembles Earth. It has a solid, rocky surface that a spacecraft could land on. Pictures of Mars show us that it is very cold and there are ice caps at its poles, like on Earth. It also has seasons and days similar to those on our planet.

5…4…3…2…1. We have liftoff! What forces are at play when a rocket is launched into space? Read on to find out.

Mars is often called the Red Planet because its surface is covered in red rocks and sand and not much else. They are red because the planet contains a lot of iron oxide, or rust.

FORCES AND MOTION

A force is a push or a pull—something that makes an object move, change speed, or change shape. No matter how hard we push against the ground, we can't get very high above it unless we use a trampoline or a jet pack! For a rocket to lift off into space, its engines have to create an enormous and powerful force.

What Do Space Rockets Do?

Space rockets are powerful vehicles that fly from Earth to space. They are often used to launch satellites or space probes. Rockets have very powerful engines. They need a lot of force to speed away from our planet and escape its **gravity** or they would fall back down to Earth.

Gravity

Earth is so big that it pulls everything on or near its surface toward its center. This downward pull is the force of gravity. It is the force that pulls you back to the ground every time you jump. The pulling force of gravity is also what gives you and everything else on Earth **weight**. Your weight is how heavy you are. An object with a large **mass** is heavier because it is pulled more than a small mass. So, a giant space rocket is much, much harder to lift off the ground than you!

Thrust

When a rocket is waiting on a launchpad, gravity is pulling it downward. However, an equal force is pushing it upward (the support force of the ground). These forces are **balanced**, so the rocket does not move. Objects only move when forces acting on them are **unbalanced**: when the forces pushing in one direction are greater than the forces pushing in the opposite direction. **Thrust** is a pushing or pulling force that makes an object move. For a rocket to take off and shoot upward, it needs to create a thrust force that is greater than the weight of the rocket.

PAIRED FORCES

Forces always work in pairs. For example, you push backward on a skateboard and it moves forward. This is because the force from the ground on your foot is transferred into the motion of the board. This is called action and reaction. A rocket pushes exhaust gases backward and, in turn, the exhaust gases push forward on the rocket.

When thrust forces pushing a rocket upward are stronger than the gravity forces pulling it downward, the rocket will lift off.

gravity

thrust

How do rocket engines work?

Firework rockets contain gunpowder, which makes hot gases when you light it on fire. When these gases shoot downward out of a hole, the firework shoots up into the air. Space rockets work in a similar way, although they burn hundreds of tons of **fuel** to achieve liftoff.

Thrust power

To give the rocket a brief but strong burst of thrust force, the rocket engine burns a lot of fuel in a short time. Rocket fuels are solid or liquid, or a combination of the two. When this fuel is burned inside an enclosed space called a combustion chamber, it turns into very hot gases. At the rear of the chamber is a hole called an exhaust nozzle. The hot gases shoot out of the nozzle into the air behind them. As the gases are pushed out of the back, they create a thrust force that pushes the rocket upward.

Full of fuel

Rocket launchers weigh hundreds of tons at liftoff. Most of this weight is fuel. The fuel needed to launch a rocket into space usually weighs about 20 times more than the rocket itself. The speed of a rocket depends on how much fuel is burned per second. To go fast, rockets burn thousands of gallons of fuel a second. The speed at which a rocket moves also depends on its mass. Lighter rockets will **accelerate** (speed up) faster than heavier ones using the same thrust, so scientists try to put in only the fuel that a rocket will need, to keep the rocket as light as possible.

POWER BOOSTERS

Many modern rockets have a main engine as well as two shorter booster rockets strapped to the side. These give the rocket an extra push at the beginning of its flight. After the boosters have used up all their fuel, they are detached from the rocket and land safely in oceans or on remote parts of Earth.

reaction

The action of the gases pushing backward from the rocket causes a reaction in the opposite direction, and the rocket is pushed forward

thrust

Thrust occurs when the push from the exhaust is greater than the pull of gravity

gravity

In a rocket, thrust is created by the force of gases from burning rocket fuel.

burning fuel ------->

nozzle -------->

hot exhaust gas ---->
escaping at high
speed

action

ACTIVITY: Build a Rocket

Create a rocket using the air inside a balloon for thrust. You could even get your friends to make their own and then set up a balloon rocket race!

You will need:
- a long, thin balloon
- a long piece of smooth string (about 33 ft., or 10 m, long)
- a drinking straw
- a clothespin
- masking tape
- two chairs

Optional extras:
- coins
- a stopwatch
- a tape measure

1 Blow up the balloon and secure the open end using the clothespin so no air can escape for the moment.

2 Use a few pieces of tape to attach the straw down the length of the balloon.

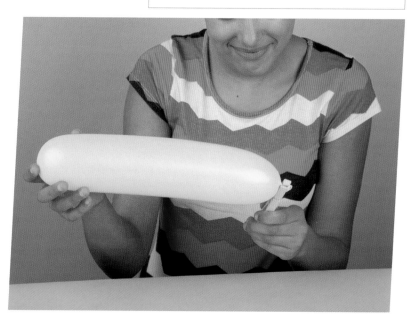

3 Thread the string through the straw and run it from a start to a finish point— for example, between the backs of two chairs.

4 Stand the chairs far apart and then use tape to securely attach each end of the string to the backs of the chairs.

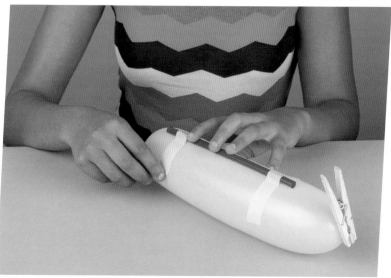

5 Now, take off the clothespin so the air can escape from the balloon. What happens?

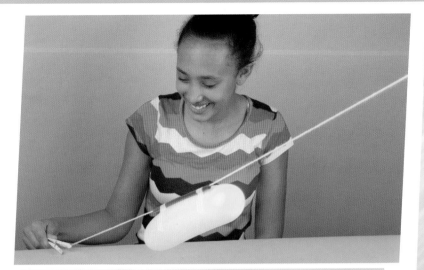

Conclusion

The thrust force comes from the balloon forcing the air out. As the air rushes out of the balloon, it pushes the rocket forward. The action is the air shooting out, and the reaction is the rocket moving forward.

TRY THIS!

Now that you have made a rocket, try some experiments with it. Try launching it upward or see what happens when you add extra weight—for example, by taping some coins to it. What do you think will happen if you only half-inflate the balloon, so there is less air in it to start with? You could use the stopwatch and tape measure to record how fast and far the rocket travels. How did your predictions compare with the results?

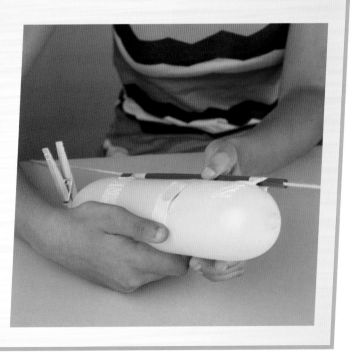

Why Do Astronauts Feel Heavy after Takeoff?

As the rocket races upward, astronauts inside a spacecraft are pushed back hard against their seats. Their bodies feel very heavy and they find it hard to move their arms. What's happening?

acceleration

gravity

At takeoff, astronauts lie flat on their backs because this is the best position in which to bear the g-forces of acceleration due to the launch.

SAME MASS, DIFFERENT WEIGHT

People often confuse mass and weight. The mass of an object is how much **matter** there is in it. We measure mass in pounds or kilograms, but when we say we weigh an amount in pounds or kilograms, we are not being very accurate! Strictly speaking, the weight of an object is the gravitational force between the object and Earth and it is measured in **Newtons**. The mass of astronauts stays the same wherever they go, but their weight changes if gravity changes.

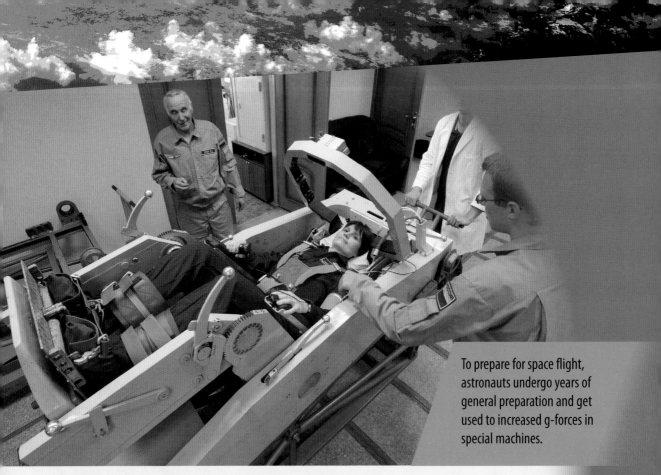

To prepare for space flight, astronauts undergo years of general preparation and get used to increased g-forces in special machines.

Feeling heavy

G-force is a measure of how much force acts on a person or an object compared with the normal weight force due to Earth's gravity. You are feeling it right now. While you sit and read this, you are experiencing a g-force of 1 g. You don't notice this g-force because you are used to it acting on you all the time. We only notice gravity forces when they increase; for example, you might have noticed gentle g-forces when taking off in an airplane. It feels like something is pushing you backward.

Feel the force!

Astronauts experience a g-force of about 4.5 g as they take off and fly through Earth's **atmosphere**. Because the rocket is accelerating through the atmosphere, astronauts feel a strong pull downward that feels like gravity. The body's fluids also weigh more, so the heart has to pump faster to push blood all the way to the brain. This can cause astronauts to become dizzy or even, in extreme cases, to pass out (faint). So, astronauts wear special suits and have to train in high g-forces.

Why Are Rockets Long and Thin?

Rockets accelerate to speeds of up to 17,400 mph (28,000 km/h)!

fins

Rockets are long and thin to help them move faster. When objects move through the sky, they push against the air around them, and this slows them down. This **air resistance** is what makes it hard to move forward when we walk into the wind. There is less air resistance on thinner shapes than wider ones because a smaller surface area is pushing against the air. That's why racing cyclists lean down to make a more **streamlined** shape to go faster.

Fins for flight

Some rockets have fins on their tail end. These use air resistance to keep the rocket steady and traveling in the right direction while it is in Earth's atmosphere. Air presses against both sides of the fins with equal force when the rocket is flying straight. But if the rocket tilts to the right or left, there is more force on one side of the fin than the other side. This pushes the tail of the rocket back into line.

FRICTION

Air resistance is a form of **friction** between air and another material. Friction is a force between two surfaces that are moving against each other. Friction slows moving objects down. Friction is greater on rougher surfaces because there are more bumps and edges to rub and catch against. Spacecraft have very smooth surfaces, to reduce friction with the air.

thrust

drag

lower drag at tip

drag

higher drag at tail

Fins on rockets work in the same way as feathers on the tails of arrows. The greater drag on the feathers keeps the tail at the back, so the point of the arrow travels straight forward.

How Do Spacecraft Orbit Earth?

Beyond Earth's atmosphere, there is almost no air, and the force of gravity is weaker than near the surface. Flying in space has many advantages over flying in our atmosphere. Without air in space, there is no air resistance to slow spacecraft down, so they continue moving fast. However, spacecraft have to take their own supplies of **oxygen** for the engines to use. Without air, there is also nothing for fins to push against to steer.

Flying around Earth

Spacecraft would fall gradually toward Earth because of its weak gravitational pull, even on objects high above the surface. But they often stay the same height above its surface, flying on a circular path around the globe. This is called an **orbit**. Spacecraft can orbit because they are moving so fast. The faster an object travels, the more horizontal distance it covers as it falls, and the gentler the curve of its path. Throw a ball softly, and it arcs to the ground near you because of gravity. Throw it as hard as you can, and it flies straight for longer before falling. If you could throw that ball at 17,000 miles (27,359 kilometers) per hour, the curve of its path would match the curve of Earth, so it would remain at the same distance from Earth. To stay in orbit, spacecraft must fly at this speed or faster.

ORBIT SPEED

The speed needed to stay in orbit depends on the height a spacecraft is above Earth. This is because the pull of gravity is slightly stronger nearer to Earth. So, a craft just above Earth's atmosphere must fly at around 5 miles (8 kilometers) each second. Farther away from Earth, the speed drops. Orbiting spacecraft overtake each other by lowering their orbit. One fires **thruster** rockets forward to slow down. This makes it drop into a lower orbit, where it travels faster and overtakes the other spacecraft!

Without gravity, the spacecraft would keep moving into outer space in a straight line. Gravity changes the craft's straight motion into a circular orbit.

gravity

satellite orbit

travel in a straight line

Gravity acts in space just as it does on Earth. A spacecraft needs to fly at least 17,000 mph (27,359 km/h) to beat gravity.

But if it is slower than that, it will fall back to Earth

gravity

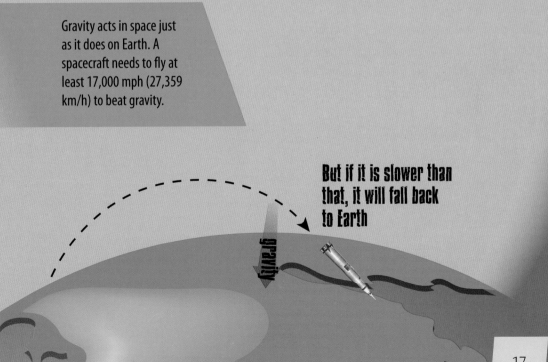

There are more than 1,100 satellites orbiting Earth, carrying out a variety of useful tasks for people living on our planet.

Which spacecraft orbit Earth?

Most spacecraft that orbit Earth are satellites. They got into space inside rockets, so they are mostly the size of a car or smaller, though they are bigger once unfolded. Satellites are not streamlined like rockets, because they do not have to travel through the atmosphere. They often have antennae, **solar panels** to generate electricity from sunlight, and other parts sticking out. Satellites all have instruments that allow them to communicate with Earth. Weather satellites, for example, use equipment to record the movement of clouds over Earth and help us predict the weather.

Biggest satellite

The International Space Station is the biggest satellite in space. Astronauts from around the world live and work there for weeks at a time. The station was assembled by astronauts using parts carried from Earth on different missions because the whole satellite is far too big for one rocket to carry. The parts include solar panels, living compartments, and science laboratories where scientists carry out experiments in space. Other important parts include small spacecraft that astronauts can use to escape and get to Earth if there is an emergency.

Some satellites are the size of a toaster oven, but the International Space Station is the size of a football field and weighs around 462 tons!

ORBITING DANGER

It is not just spaceships that orbit Earth, but also space junk left by people. Scientists estimate that there are about 21,000 pieces over 4 inches (10 centimeters) long orbiting Earth. They include parts of exploded rockets, discarded after taking satellites to space, and tools accidentally dropped by astronauts. Space junk is a problem because it can fly into and damage or even blast a hole through a spacecraft!

On the space station, the crew members work to maintain the craft and carry out science experiments, but after that, they eat, sleep, and relax as we do on Earth. However, life on a space station is different from life on Earth in one major way. In space, astronauts don't walk around inside their spacecraft—they float!

Falling with style

Astronauts orbiting Earth in a space station feel **weightless**. Even though they are far from Earth, this is not because of a lack of gravity. The space station is held in orbit because of the pull of Earth's gravity. Astronauts only appear to be floating when, in fact, they are falling. They and the space station are falling together, so it looks like the astronauts are floating!

Astronauts train for zero gravity in a machine known as a vomit comet. Can you guess why?!

Daily life

Being weightless changes daily life. Astronauts have to attach themselves to their beds in sleeping bags so that they don't float around and bump into things. They have to strap themselves to a toilet that has a special device for sucking away waste. They eat some of the same foods, but often in packaging that stops it from floating away. One advantage of being weightless is that it is easy to move heavy objects—you can move things that weigh hundreds of pounds with the tips of your fingers!

ZERO GRAVITY

When we drop a book on Earth, we see it fall. If an astronaut drops the same book inside a space station, it looks like the book floats rather than falls. Because the book, the astronaut, and the space station are all in orbit, falling toward Earth together, the book has become weightless. It appears to float in the state we call zero gravity or **microgravity**.

Why do astronauts use exercise bikes?

Astronauts use a variety of exercise equipment for at least two hours every day. This isn't just to make sure they can fit into their space suits! Astronauts must exercise hard every day to prevent bone and muscle loss.

Muscle and bone loss

On Earth, our bodies are constantly working against the force of gravity. Apart from when we are lying down in bed asleep, our muscles and bones have to support our own body weight all day long. In space, astronauts experience weightlessness, and the body does not need to work to support and move them. This means their bones and muscles could get weaker. This would reduce their strength and ability to work, stand up straight, and walk back on Earth. But microgravity means astronauts get taller after spending months in space. That's because discs between the bones in their spines are crushed less, as they have less weight to support.

The space gym

Astronauts use a variety of exercise machines. They walk, jog, or run on a treadmill. They are attached to this with harnesses that pull them down to the walking surface with a force equal to their body weight. The bike they ride is an ergometer, which is like a bicycle without wheels. They can adjust it so that their legs have to work and push harder. They also use a type of weight-lifting machine to give themselves a workout.

FORCES AND EXERCISE

We should all exercise to keep our muscles and bones strong and healthy. The best exercises for bones and muscles are called **weight-bearing exercises** because they work against gravity. Examples of weight-bearing exercises include hiking, jogging, climbing stairs, tennis, and dancing.

body reaction force against bungee

Astronauts wear harnesses attached to bungees when they use the treadmill. The bungees stop them from floating off and also create a downward load to push against.

simulated forward motion

ground reaction force against treadmill

force through bungee

gravity

treadmill direction

ACTIVITY: Measuring G-Forces

G-forces on astronauts change greatly from takeoff on rockets through to life on space stations. Make a device to measure the g-forces you feel when you change your motion.

You will need:
- a cardboard tube 2 in. (5 cm) in diameter and 12 in. (30 cm) long
- two rubber bands about 2 in. (5 cm) long
- three identical steel nuts (each weighing about 1 oz., or 30 g)
- two paper clips
- scissors
- sticky tape
- felt-tip marker

SAFETY! Wear safety goggles for this activity. They'll protect your eyes if the rubber band snaps and the nut flies off.

1 With an adult's help, carefully measure, mark, and cut a window ¾ in. (2 cm) wide and 8 in. (20 cm) long in the center of the tube.

2 Straighten one paper clip. Bend it over the end of the tube and use tape to secure. Cut each rubber band in half and tie both bands together. Tie one end of the long rubber band to the center of the paper clip bar across the tube.

3 Repeat step 2 for the other end of the tube, but tie one nut to the middle of the band before tying off the other end.

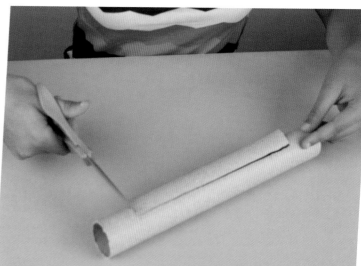

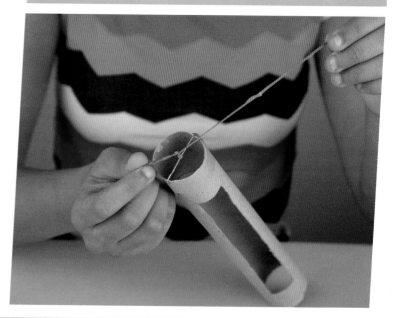

4 Stand the tube upright and mark the side of the tube where the nut stays as "1 G." Temporarily tape a second nut to the first. The extra mass of the second nut should pull the rubber band down. Mark the new position of the first nut as "2 G." Repeat with the third nut and mark the new position as "3 G." Remove the second and third nuts.

5 Turn the tube upside down and repeat step 4. This time, mark the nut positions as "−1 G," "−2 G," and "−3 G."

6 At the middle of the tube, halfway between "1 G" and "−1 G," mark the position "0 G." Your accelerometer is ready!

TRY THIS!

See what measurement your accelerometer shows when you:
- pretend to throw the tube to the ground
- are in an elevator
- are on a roller coaster at an amusement park (if you can get to one).

What g-forces did you experience?

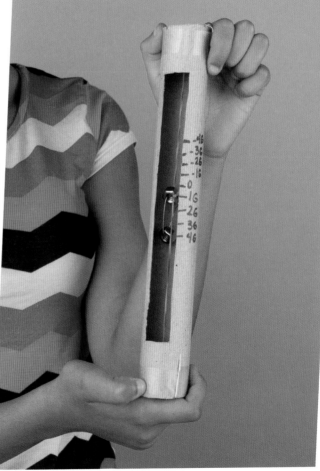

When an astronaut gets out of the spacecraft while it is in space, this is known as a **spacewalk**. Astronauts go on spacewalks for various reasons. They set up science experiments on the outside of a spacecraft to study how being in space affects different things. They repair satellites or spacecraft and they test new equipment.

Keeping safe

In space, astronauts have to be tied to the spacecraft to stop them from floating away. Safety tethers are like very strong ropes with metal clips: one end is attached to the astronaut, the other to the spacecraft. These tethers help them stay close to their spacecraft. Astronauts also have to attach their tools to their space suits to stop them from floating away.

A spacewalk is also called an EVA. "EVA" stands for "extravehicular activity."

WEIGHTLESS IN WATER

Astronauts train for spacewalks underwater in a giant swimming pool, because working underwater is similar to working outside in space. For every hour that astronauts spend on a spacewalk, they will have spent seven hours training in the pool, working on replica satellites and spacecraft.

Jet packs

Another way astronauts stay safe during spacewalks is by wearing a SAFER (Simplified Aid for Extravehicular Activity Rescue). The SAFER is like a jet pack, equipped with 24 mini thruster jets. If astronauts were to become detached and float away from the space station, they can use their SAFER jet pack to fly back. The push of gases away from the thruster jets produces an equal and opposite push on the SAFER. Astronauts can control which thrusters fire, helping them move around in space.

The SAFER's control unit is a box on a tether. The astronaut uses a device that is a bit like a video game controller to operate its thrusters.

Why do astronauts wear space suits?

Astronauts have to wear special space suits to go on a spacewalk. This is because space is a very dangerous place.

Astronauts never go outside without a space suit called an Extravehicular Mobility Unit (EMU). A space suit is like an astronaut's personal spacecraft because it contains all an astronaut needs to survive. In space, it can get burning hot when you face the Sun and freezing cold in the shade, so EMUs have layers of **insulation**. Pumps circulate warm or cool fluid through pipes to control an astronaut's temperature. Fingers are the parts of the body that get coldest in space, so the gloves have heated fingertips. Tough outer layers protect astronauts from getting hurt—tiny pieces of space junk can move faster than a bullet when orbiting in space. Most helmets have gold-lined **visors** to reflect bright sunlight away from an astronaut's eyes.

The backpack

The space suit backpack contains oxygen so astronauts can breathe. Because there is no air in space, there is no push from gases or **air pressure**. A fan in the backpack moves oxygen through the space suit so that oxygen is constantly pressing against the astronaut's skin. This keeps the air pressure around the body the same as it would be on Earth, and that is why space suits look so puffed up. Without the air pressure the astronauts are used to, their blood would boil, their skin and organs would swell up, and then they would freeze!

AIR PRESSURE

Air has weight that we call air pressure. Air pressure is different on different parts of Earth. It is greater at sea level, where the full weight of air in the atmosphere weighs down on us. If you climb a mountain, there is less air pressure. We don't feel the weight of all that air pushing down on us because our bodies contain air that pushes outward so that these forces are balanced.

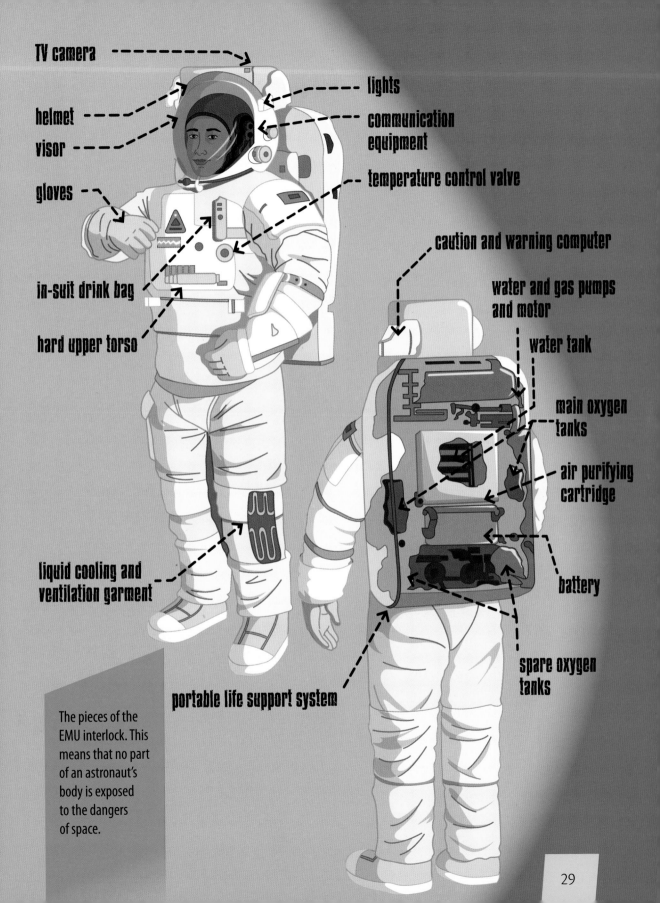

TV camera

lights

helmet

communication equipment

visor

temperature control valve

gloves

caution and warning computer

water and gas pumps and motor

water tank

in-suit drink bag

main oxygen tanks

hard upper torso

air purifying cartridge

battery

liquid cooling and ventilation garment

spare oxygen tanks

portable life support system

The pieces of the EMU interlock. This means that no part of an astronaut's body is exposed to the dangers of space.

How Do Spacecraft Go Farther?

Mars is at least 34.8 million miles (56 million kilometers) away from Earth. Even today's fastest spacecraft would take about six months to get there. It would take a huge amount of fuel, oxygen, and other supplies to transport astronauts that far and back. However, scientists have found quicker ways to send unmanned spacecraft to Mars with the assistance of gravity.

Different orbits

Imagine you were riding on a Ferris wheel and your friend was spinning on a merry-go-round next to it at an amusement park. During the rides, you would be farther or closer together at different times. Earth and Mars have different shapes and directions of orbits around the Sun, so the distance between the two planets changes all throughout the year—just like the distance between you and your friend! Scientists can plan spacecraft journeys to take advantage of the effects of gravity when the two planets are closest together.

Gravity assist

The way spacecraft can use different orbit paths to hop between planets is called **gravity assist**. The spacecraft orbits Earth and then accelerates to leave the orbit at a particular moment. Earth's gravity gives it more energy and flings it on a new orbit. The timing and speed are carefully calculated so that the spacecraft can meet up with Mars on that planet's own orbit path.

SOLAR SYSTEM

Our planet is part of a group of planets called the solar system that revolve around the Sun. The Sun is 743 times bigger than all the planets put together; it makes up over 99 percent of the total mass of everything in our solar system. This is why it has such a great gravitational pull on all the planets. However, just like satellites around Earth, the planets are traveling so fast that they stay in orbit rather than fall into the Sun.

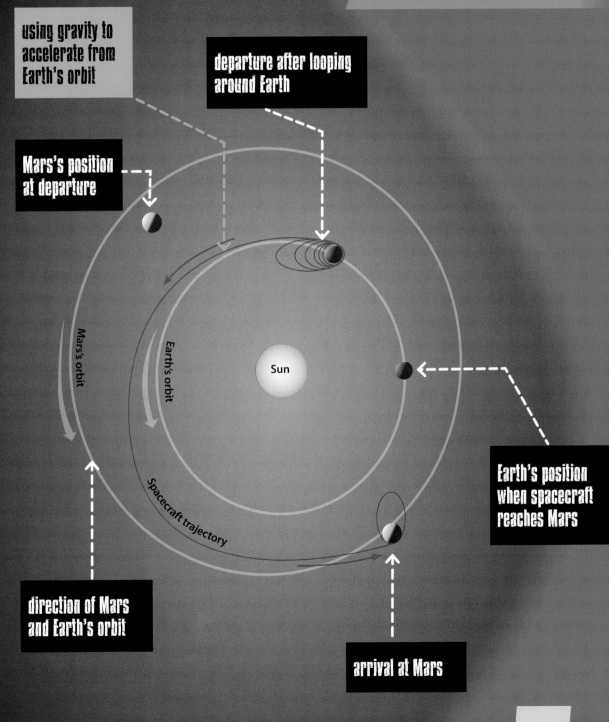

Spacecraft can use Earth's gravity and orbit around the Sun like a slingshot to push them into Mars's orbit. This uses less fuel and takes less time than flying directly on their own power.

using gravity to accelerate from Earth's orbit

departure after looping around Earth

Mars's position at departure

Mars's orbit

Earth's orbit

Sun

Spacecraft trajectory

Earth's position when spacecraft reaches Mars

direction of Mars and Earth's orbit

arrival at Mars

After being accelerated through space toward Mars by gravity assist, spacecraft are directed toward the chosen landing place on the surface. But entry into the Martian atmosphere is a great challenge because of the forces the spacecraft encounters.

Cruising and preparing

In the months leading up to arrival on Mars, spacecraft cruise along while instruments inside are busy. Some systems check everything is functioning properly on board the spacecraft in preparation for landing. The location of the spacecraft is monitored at all times by a mission team using computers back on Earth. The team sends radio signals to operate thrusters, which adjust the craft's course. This makes sure the spacecraft meets Mars at the right place. It also aims the craft's solar panels toward the Sun, so it can generate power.

Dangerous entry

The spacecraft is flying at 12,000 miles (19,300 kilometers) per hour when it first enters the Martian atmosphere nearly 7 miles (about 11 kilometers) above the surface. The craft's downward force and the pull of gravity from Mars produce an equal and opposite force of friction against the gases in the atmosphere rubbing against its flat underside. Air resistance, or drag, slows the craft. But friction also produces dangerously hot temperatures of up to 3,800 degrees Fahrenheit (2,100 degrees Celsius)—about four times hotter than a pizza oven! Luckily, the spacecraft has a thick plate called a **heat shield** underneath that protects its instruments and cargo from the high temperatures.

ENERGY CHANGES

Energy never disappears—it just changes form. Switch on a light and some of the electrical energy turns to light energy. The speeding spacecraft has lots of movement or **kinetic energy**. Friction from the Martian atmosphere reduces the kinetic energy in the spacecraft as it slows from 3.7 to 0.28 miles per second (5.9 to 0.45 kilometers per second). But this energy changes into heat energy that warms up the heat shield.

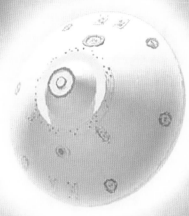

On entry into the Martian atmosphere, the heat shield on a spacecraft glows red-hot or even produces flames as gases in the atmosphere burn.

Parachutes for spacecraft are made from tough materials similar to Kevlar, which is used to make bulletproof vests.

How does a spacecraft slow down?

The spacecraft is now running out of time to slow down and avoid crashing into Mars. But it has ways of producing more drag to reduce speed over the remaining distance. The first is by leaning, so that the air flows faster on top than underneath. The second is by releasing a **parachute**. Parachutes produce drag in response to gravity by increasing the surface area that air can push against. A parachute makes the spacecraft's speed fall to 9 percent of the speed it was moving at when it reached Mars's atmosphere.

AIR BAG LANDING

Earlier spacecraft landed on Mars using protective air bags like those used in cars—but much bigger! Just seconds before impact, 24 air bags inflated around a pod containing a Mars rover. It looked like a big bunch of grapes! After hitting the ground, it bounced the height of a four-story building and then bounced over 20 more times until it came to a rest. The cushioning absorbed the upward force from the ground and protected the pod from damage.

Light landing

About 5 miles (8 kilometers) from landing, the spacecraft gets rid of some mass so that there is less for Mars's gravity to pull on. It gets rid of its heat shield and the parachute. The spacecraft free-falls and then switches on its downward thrusters. This produces more lift, but the thrusters must not be fired too soon or they will run out of fuel before landing. If fired too late, the thrusters won't slow the spacecraft down. Finally, the remaining part of the spacecraft, called a sky crane, hovers above Mars's surface. This lowers the **rover**—a Mars exploration vehicle—down on ropes before flying away.

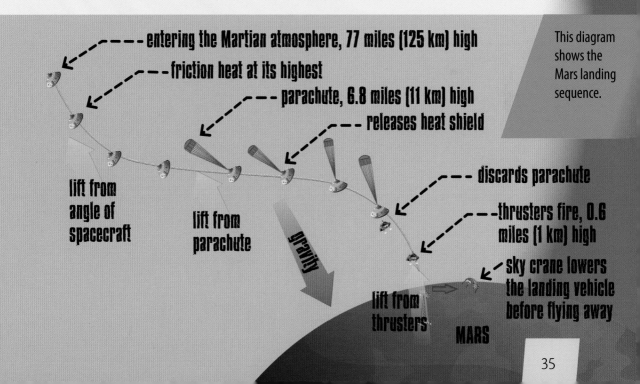

entering the Martian atmosphere, 77 miles (125 km) high

friction heat at its highest

parachute, 6.8 miles (11 km) high

releases heat shield

discards parachute

thrusters fire, 0.6 miles (1 km) high

sky crane lowers the landing vehicle before flying away

lift from angle of spacecraft

lift from parachute

gravity

lift from thrusters

MARS

This diagram shows the Mars landing sequence.

ACTIVITY: Eggstronaut Survivor

Mars missions rely partly on parachutes to land safely. Make a landing craft to carry an eggstronaut from one story high down to the ground without cracking!

SAFETY! Make sure an adult is with you when you carry out this experiment and remember to wash your hands after handling eggs.

You will need:
- 6 fresh eggs
- felt-tip marker
- 2 plastic sandwich bags
- black trash bag
- scissors
- hole punch
- string
- stopwatch
- bubble wrap

1 Get artistic! Draw the face of an astronaut on an egg. Place the egg in a sandwich bag and knot the top.

2 Use scissors to cut a 4-in. (10-cm) square of black trash bag. Use the hole punch to make a hole in each corner and tie the end of a 12-in. (30-cm) piece of string on each hole. Tie the other ends of the string tightly to the top of the sandwich bag.

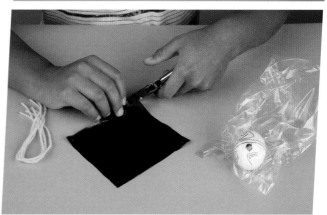

3 If you have access to some stairs, go to the top of the first flight and, being careful not to lean over the rail, hold out the top of the parachute attached to the egg. Get a helper to operate the stopwatch and time the egg's descent to the floor. Was the egg damaged? Repeat twice to get several fall times.

4 Repeat steps 2 and 3 but with a 12-in. (30-cm) parachute (and a different egg and bag if the first egg broke). Did the egg fall faster or slower?

5 Retest the small parachute, covering the egg in bubble wrap before putting it in the sandwich bag.

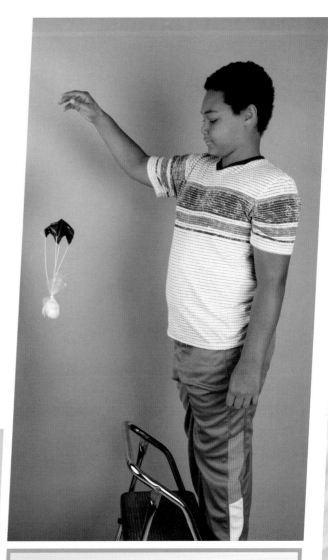

Conclusion

When you drop the egg, gravity pulling on the egg pulls on the strings. This opens the parachute, creating a large surface area and more air resistance to slow the egg's fall. Larger parachutes slow the fall more than small parachutes because their surface areas are bigger. Bubble wrap acts like air bags on a Mars lander by cushioning the upward force on the egg from the floor.

TRY THIS!
- Measure the height of the drop and figure out the average falling speed in feet per second.

- Test other protective carriers for eggs, such as pieces of egg carton, feathers, or balloons. You could also try other materials and sizes of parachutes.

How Do Rovers Drive on Mars?

After landing on Mars, a rover starts its journey over the surface. Rovers are car-sized robots that are steered and controlled using computers on Earth. The rover is designed to explore Mars for about three months, collecting, grinding, and analyzing samples of soil and rock.

Mars rover Curiosity is a six-wheeled robot equipped with lots of instruments for studying the planet in detail.

mast with cameras helping scientists on Earth see where it's going and what it's doing

hinged suspension so rover can absorb force from bumps

forward thrust caused by backward push from tire tread on the ground

gravity weaker than on Earth

reaction force from ground resulting from gravity

On the move

The rover's six large wheels have thick treads, or grooves, to increase friction. This helps it climb over the rocks and prevents it from slipping on sand. Each wheel also has its own motor to move the rover in all directions. The rover does not need huge amounts of power to move. Mars has a thin atmosphere, and there is far less air resistance on Mars than there is on Earth for the rover to push against. This means it does not have to accelerate as much.

A bumpy surface

The rover also has a suspension system to help it drive over the rough, rocky surface without toppling. The wheels are connected to and interact with the rover body in a way that absorbs some of the impact when the rover hits a bump, just as suspension systems do on cars. The difference is that gravity on Mars is weaker than it is on Earth, so the rover weighs much less on Mars than it does on Earth. This means its suspension system can be weaker than it would be on Earth.

UPS AND DOWNS

When a vehicle hits a bump in a road, this thrusts the wheel into the air. As a wheel is pushed up, the whole vehicle could be pushed up off the ground, too. The reaction to this action could be that the force of gravity pulls the vehicle back down onto the road with an impact that could damage it. A vehicle's suspension system supports its weight and absorbs that shock, to keep the wheels on the road.

Will People Go to Mars One Day?

One of the reasons why robots such as the rover explore Mars is to see if people will be able to go there one day. Human travel to Mars is impossible today. A rocket would have to be so huge to carry all the fuel and supplies needed for the journey there and back that it would not be able to take off, even with the biggest engines now available!

Feel the forces

Space agencies have serious hopes of sending a mission to land people on Mars by the 2030s. To do so, they have to overcome and make use of a variety of forces. First, they have to create enough thrust to overcome gravity and continue on into space. They have to use planets' gravitational forces to accelerate past and leap efficiently between planets. They also have to counteract the friction and air resistance that slow spacecraft leaving Earth and use these forces to help land on Mars. Finally, they will need to cope with microgravity and the harsh environment of space.

Life on Mars

If people do make it to Mars in the future, there would need to be several spacecraft involved to take the supplies they would need. Scientists are working on ways to collect water from ice on the planet. This would be used for drinking water and to make oxygen. The atmosphere on Mars is mostly made of carbon dioxide, so they would need to make oxygen to breathe. Other scientists are designing buildings to protect people from the cold temperatures. They would need to find ways to melt the ice on Mars to make the liquid water they need so that they could grow plants to feed themselves. A Dutch company, Mars One, is already asking for volunteers to join a one-way trip to Mars in the future. Would you go?

This is an artist's reconstruction of what a future settlement on Mars might look like.

Quiz

1 Which force pulls us down when we jump up?
   a) friction
   b) thrust
   c) gravity
   d) weight

2 What is the word we use to describe when two forces are equal?
   a) balanced
   b) unbalanced
   c) uneven
   d) pairs of forces

3 Which of these statements is false about gravity?
   a) Gravity is stronger the closer together two objects are.
   b) Gravity is larger when the mass of an object is larger.
   c) Gravity only exists between large objects.
   d) Gravity gets less the farther two objects are apart.

4 Which of these statements is false about weight and mass?
   a) Weight is a force caused by gravity.
   b) Mass is the amount of matter an object is made from.
   c) The mass of an object stays the same wherever it is, but its weight can change.
   d) Weight is measured in grams. Mass is measured in Newtons.

5 What causes a rocket to move?
   a) The engines push against the vacuum of space.
   b) The rocket pushes away from gravity.
   c) The exhaust gases push forward onto the rocket.
   d) It keeps moving because there are no other forces.

6 What happens to the weight of astronauts when they reach orbit from Earth compared to their weight on the surface of Earth?
- a) It stays the same.
- b) They lose weight.
- c) They gain weight.
- d) They become weightless.

7 What causes some objects to fall slower than other objects?
- a) gravity
- b) acceleration
- c) forces
- d) air resistance

8 The atmosphere on Mars is mostly made of which gas?
- a) oxygen
- b) carbon dioxide
- c) nitrogen
- d) helium

9 Which of the following do not orbit around planets?
- a) satellites
- b) planets
- c) space junk
- d) moons

10 Why will astronauts' bones and muscles become weaker if they spend a long time in a space station and don't exercise?
- a) because gravity stretches their bones and muscles
- b) because they eat different foods
- c) because gravity is too low to put normal stresses on bones and muscles
- d) because they go on spacewalks

Glossary

accelerate move more quickly; speed up

air pressure force or weight of air pressing against something

air resistance force that slows down the movement of an object through the air

atmosphere layer of different gases that surrounds a planet and is held in place by gravity

balanced when two forces acting on an object are equal in size but act in opposite directions, we say that they are balanced forces

force a push or pull on an object. A force gives energy to an object.

friction force produced when one surface moves over another surface. Friction acts to slow down the movement.

fuel material that makes heat or power, such as oil or coal

g-force measure of how much force acts on a person or an object compared with the normal weight force, due to Earth's gravity

gravity force of attraction between two objects. On Earth, gravity pulls everything toward the ground. This is because Earth's mass is much greater than everything around it.

gravity assist when a spacecraft uses the gravity of a planet to speed up, slow down, or change direction

heat shield device or coating to protect something from high temperatures that could damage or destroy it

insulation material that stops heat or cold from passing through it

kinetic energy energy a moving object has because it is moving

mass amount of matter, or physical substance, something has. Weight is related to mass because weight measures the force of gravity on the mass of an object.

matter physical substance

microgravity very weak gravity

Newton unit of force used to measure the strength of a push or a pull

orbit path one object in space takes around another

oxygen gas that is needed for something to burn

parachute large piece of material that unfolds and uses air resistance to slow down someone or something's descent through the air

resource supply of something useful, such as air, water, or fuel

rover space vehicle that can be driven over rough terrain, guided by remote control

satellite electronic device placed in orbit around Earth. Weather satellites are used to collect weather information, and communications satellites pass on TV and radio signals.

solar panel panel that uses the energy in sunlight to make electricity

spacewalk when an astronaut gets out of a spacecraft while it is in space

streamlined shaped so that air or water move easily around an object

thrust force that moves an object forward

thruster machine used to make spacecraft and other vehicles move

unbalanced when one force acting on an object is greater in size than the other force, we say that they are unbalanced forces

visor part of a helmet that shields the eyes

weight gravitational force between an object and Earth

weight-bearing exercise any activity you do while on your feet and legs that works your muscles and bones against gravity

weightless floating feeling people get when there is no force of support on their body

Books

Ballard, Carol. *Exploring Forces and Movement* (How Does Science Work?). New York: PowerKids, 2008.

Claybourne, Anna. *Gut-Wrenching Gravity and Other Fatal Forces* (Disgusting and Dreadful Science). St. Catharines, Ont.: Crabtree, 2013.

Claybourne, Anna. *Make It Zoom!* (Whiz Kid Science). Chicago: Raintree, 2015.

Dicker, Katie. *Forces and Motion* (Sherlock Bones Looks at Physical Science). New York: Windmill, 2011.

Spilsbury, Louise. *Space* (Make and Learn). New York: PowerKids, 2015.

Web sites

FactHound offers a safe, fun way to find Internet sites related to this book. All of the sites on FactHound have been researched by our staff.

Here's all you do:

Visit www.facthound.com

Type in this code: 9781484626009

Places to visit

Smithsonian National Air and Space Museum
Independence Avenue at 6th Street, SW
Washington, D.C. 20560
airandspace.si.edu

The Smithsonian National Air and Space Museum has an extensive collection of objects and interactive exhibits dedicated to the history of space exploration.

Space Center Houston
1601 NASA Parkway
Houston, Texas 77058
spacecenter.org

This is the official visitor center connected to NASA's Johnson Space Center.

Further research

- Forces play an important part in flying any object—including paper airplanes. Research flight forces and use your knowledge of how they work to improve how far a paper airplane will fly.

- Research the history of space and travel. Try to find out what people mean by the "space race." Who was the first person in space, and what did the first person to land on the Moon do and say?

- Isaac Newton was a famous scientist of the 17th century who came up with three laws of motion. Find out what they are and find examples of how they work in space just as well as they do on Earth.

- Learn about the planets making up our solar system. Make a table giving their sizes, types of atmosphere, temperatures, and how strong their pull of gravity is relative to Earth. Which planets have been visited by spacecraft, and which would you like to visit most and least?

Index